TIMES PAS

-THE-
PEAK DISTRICT

This book is part of the Times Past series,
produced using photographs from the archives of the Hulton Picture Library
*including many from the famous **Picture Post** magazine.*

Top: CHATSWORTH HOUSE, 1900. Left: SHROVETIDE FOOTBALL, ASHBOURNE 1928.
Right: HIKERS IN WINNATS PASS, 1962.

MYRIAD
LONDON

BUXTON AND THE NORTHERN PEAK

The elegant spa of Buxton is England's highest market town. The source of its prosperity is St Ann's Well whose health-giving waters have been drunk since Roman times. Today, Buxton is famous for its annual opera festival and its mineral water is marketed throughout Europe.

THE OLD HALL AND CRESCENT, *c1900*. Determined that Buxton would rival Bath in its magnificence, the Duke of Devonshire commissioned John Carr of York to build the Crescent in 1779. On the left of the Crescent, with the quaint bathchair in the foreground, is the Old Hall Hotel. It occupies the site of the former townhouse of Bess of Hardwick and her husband the Earl of Shrewsbury. Mary Queen of Scots stayed at the Old Hall when she visited Buxton in 1573. The Old Hall, which is still a magnificent hotel, is reputed to be the oldest hotel in England. ABOVE RIGHT: **THE QUADRANT,** *c1900*. Built in 1860, this is one of Buxton's busiest shopping streets.

ABOVE: At the east end of The Crescent are the **HOT** or **THERMAL BATHS**. The iron colonnade shown here was part of a major reconstruction undertaken in 1853. Within a few years, the frontage was converted into shops – five in the hot bath colonnade and six along the east side of the baths known as Devonshire Colonnade. The memorial in the roadway is a four-sided drinking fountain, restored during the 1990s.

RIGHT AND BELOW: The two photographs below show SPRING GARDENS and THE HOT or THERMAL BATHS in 1940 and 1961. In 1900, the baths were remodelled and the iron colonnades shown on page 2 were removed. In 1909 a new colonnade, shown here, was constructed but it was taken down along the front of the building in the 1960s because it had become unsafe. The Hot Baths finally closed on September 30 1963 and the building remained derelict until 1985-6 when it was converted into the Cavendish Arcade Shopping Centre. The terrace to the right of the baths is The Quadrant. Looming above the street scene is The Palace (formerly Buxton) Hotel built between 1864 and 1866. To the left is Corbar Hill where much of the stone used to build this fine town was quarried.

THE PEAKS THROUGH THE SEASONS

At over 1,000 feet above sea level, snowy winters in Buxton and its environs are frequent. The best thing is to enjoy them, and look forward to the spring!

RIGHT: **BUXTON, 1904.** A woman and child enjoy tobogganing in the snow, watched by some anxious-looking males to the right. Others wait to join the fun in the background.

BELOW: Shovelling snow, 1947: German prisoners of war clear the Whaley Bridge to Buxton road near **CHAPEL-EN-LE-FRITH**. The winter of 1947 was one of the most severe of the 20th century.

BELOW: **BUXTON, 1908.** A sleigh ride through the streets of the elegant spa town.

ABOVE: **THE CAT & FIDDLE**, *c*1935. Two gentlemen snapped making their way back to their car. At 1,690ft (515m), the Cat & Fiddle is the second highest inn in England. Located on the Buxton-Macclesfield road, now officially one of the most dangerous roads in Britain, it was built when the new turnpike was completed in 1823.

ABOVE: **BUXTON**, 1934. Fourteen-year-old Peggy Mycock is cheered by her friends for being chosen as the festival queen. She was selected from 30 girls at local "elementary" schools and will be crowned during Well Dressing week in June.

RIGHT: **MAY DAY**, 1935. Local girls take a break after dancing around the maypole. Traditionally youngsters would gather wild flowers to decorate the pole and then dance around it, holding ribbons.

Peak District at play

The mysterious caverns and glorious terrain of the Peak District is the perfect setting for adventurous and challenging pursuits.

BELOW: **BAGSHAWE CAVERN, BRADWELL, 1936.** A party of schoolboys queue up to explore the cave and examine the splendid rock formations by candlelight (BOTTOM). Bagshawe is one of the Peak District's show caves. The massive cavern was discovered accidentally by lead miners in 1806 and, a century later, a passage was dug to the main cave. Today, 96 steps lead down and guided caving trips are available.

ABOVE AND RIGHT:
INTERNATIONAL RELIABILITY TRIALS, BUXTON, 1926. Motorbikes and sidecars are put through their paces on Derbyshire's rough terrain. Reliability trials were started at a time when vehicles were much more prone to breakdowns than today. Manufacturers were keen to ensure that the public knew that their products were much more dependable than their rivals. At first, trials were carried out on flat metalled surfaces. But as vehicles became more reliable, the tests were switched to areas of rough, unsurfaced terrain preferably with long hills such as those in the Peak District.

THE WESTERN APPROACH

The Derbyshire-Cheshire boundary – the western fringe of the Peak District National Park – consists of a dramatic gritstone escarpment. In clear weather it is possible to see for miles – with luck, as far as the sea beyond the Wirral.

ABOVE: **WINTER DRIVING, JANUARY 1937**. A wintry scene west of Buxton. The snow-clad hills and absence of traffic give this photograph a dreamlike quality.

RIGHT: **SPRING HARVEST, 1945.** A beautiful shire horse pulls a waggon laden with mangolds on a Derbyshire farm. At the end of the Second World War traditional farming methods still held sway: it would be another two decades before tractors would replace heavy horses.

Above: **ECCLES PIKE, 1936.** Chapel-en-le-Frith's coronation committee decided to celebrate the coronation of King Edward VIII with the purchase of Eccles Pike, one of Derbyshire's best-known landmarks. The hill is about a mile and a half west of Chapel-en-le-Frith. At 1,213ft (370m) above sea level there are panoramic views – the Cheshire plain to the west and the Peak District to the east. The summit is now owned by the National Trust.

Right: **AUTUMN FOG, 1936.** A couple stand on a hillside above **GLOSSOP** to view the valley beneath. This historic town is sited at the foot of the Snake Pass, one of the principal routes linking Manchester and Sheffield. It is the largest town in the north-western corner of the Peak and, like Buxton, it lies just outside the boundary of the national park. Richard Arkwright's invention of the stocking frame in 1771 fuelled the expansion of Glossop: in the late 18th and early 19th centuries 46 cotton mills were built in the town. Today it is a busy commuter town serving Manchester, 12 miles to the west.

KINDER SCOUT AND THE PENNINE WAY

Britain's longest footpath, the Pennine Way, begins just above Edale in the High Peak north-east of Buxton. The path from the valley winds up to Lose Hill and the great plateau of Kinder Scout, the scene of the "mass trespass" in 1932 when five ramblers were gaoled for their part in the protest. The actions of these intrepid walkers – and others before and since – paved the way for the creation of the Peak District National Park in 1951.

> LOSE HILL 1,563 FT
> THIS SUMMIT & 54½ ACRES AROUND IT, WARD'S PIECE,
> WAS PURCHASED BY THE SHEFFIELD & DISTRICT
> FEDERATION OF THE RAMBLERS' ASSOCIATION
> IN APPRECIATION OF THE LIFE'S WORK OF
> GEORGE HERBERT BRIDGES WARD F.R.G.S.
> HE FOUNDED THE SHEFFIELD CLARION RAMBLERS
> 1900 & THE S. & D.F. 1926 & STEADFASTLY HELPED
> BY FANNIE BERTHA WARD HIS WIFE, COMMENCED THE
> GREAT RAMBLING MOVEMENT IN SHEFFIELD & DISTRICT.
> MUCH OF OUR FREEDOM ON THESE DERBYSHIRE
> MOORS & VALLEYS IS DUE TO HIS UNTIRING EFFORTS
> PRESENTED TO THE NATIONAL TRUST, IN THEIR PRESENCE 8TH APRIL 1945
> "A RAMBLER MADE IS A MAN IMPROVED"

ABOVE AND LEFT: Ramblers trekking up **LOSE HILL PIKE** and relaxing on its slopes. In May 1945 the 1,563-ft (476m) summit, together with 54 surrounding acres, were bought by Sheffield ramblers to commemorate the work of GHB Ward – the founder of the first Sunday rambling club.

INSET: The plaque which commemorates the purchase of Lose Hill Pike, which was re-named Ward's Piece. In 1900 George Herbert Bridges Ward (1876-1957) founded the **SHEFFIELD CLARION RAMBLERS**, the first working-class ramblers organisation. One of the great campaigners for the "right to roam", he was passionate about the folklore, place names and history of the Peak District. He believed that the Clarion club was the "ice-breaker and path-finder" for lovers of the outdoors and in 1945 he donated Lose Hill Pike to the National Trust. To quote from the plaque, "Much of our freedom on these Derbyshire moors & valleys is due to his untiring efforts".

RIGHT: **THE NAG'S HEAD, EDALE, 1960.** This picturesque pub is situated below the Peak on Kinder Scout and is a convenient starting point for walkers setting out on the Pennine Way.

ABOVE: **KINDER SCOUT, 1939.** Winter sports enthusiasts enjoy the rare opportunity of Alpine skiing in Derbyshire.

BELOW: **EDALE, 1938.** Young skier Tamsin Heardman sees the funny side of a fall.

From the west, the pretty village of Castleton can only be reached via the narrow limestone gorge of Winnats Pass.

ABOVE: **SPEEDWELL CAVERN, CASTLETON.** Two children sit on a wrought iron bench outside the entrance to the Speedwell Cavern. Their Edwardian dress suggests the picture was taken in the first years of the 20th century. The caves and caverns of the area are a magnet for visitors, with three main attractions – Treak Cliff, Speedwell and Peak Cavern. Speedwell can only be approached by boat, along an underground "canal" or flooded tunnel.

LEFT: **WINNATS PASS,** *c*1940. This narrow route is the only road through the steep ravine created by the limestone cliffs of the Winnats - the name possibly meaning "Gate of the Wind". It was for centuries a packhorse route between Sheffield and Cheshire, and part of it was absorbed into the new turnpike between Manchester and Sheffield, built in 1758. The view from the top of Win Hill Pike (1,518ft/462m) is one of the finest in the Peak District.

ABOVE: **MAM TOR, 1936.** This photograph was taken in November and shows the mountain and surrounding countryside bathed in sunshine when the rest of Britain was fogbound. Some 1,700ft (518m) above sea level, it is popularly known as the "Shivering Mountain" because the shale from which it is formed is unstable and and the whole hillside is gradually slipping into the valley. The summit is the highest point in the curtain of hills at the head of the Hope Valley. Its softly undulating shape gives rise to the name Mam Tor – the "mother mountain".

BELOW AND LEFT: **CASTLETON, 1960.** Two "round the corner" views of the village.

Down memory lane in Castleton

Gloriously situated at the top of the Hope Valley, Castleton is regarded as the "Gem of the Peaks". Besides boasting its splendid show caves, it is also famous for its village festivals.

Left: **Castleton, 1960.** A view from the marketplace towards Pinsdale Road, with the war memorial in the foreground.

Above: **Oak Apple Day, 1936.** This traditional village event dates back to 1660 when the Stuart monarch, Charles II, was restored to the throne after the demise of Puritan rule. It is held on May 29, and probably derives from an ancient pagan ritual to mark the end of winter. A 3ft-high garland decorated with leaves and flowers is placed on the shoulders of the "King" who is dressed in Stuart costume. He and his Queen tour the village on horseback, accompanied by a procession and band. At the end of the ceremony the garland is lifted onto the spire of St Edmund's Church and the Queen's wreath is placed on the war memorial. This is followed by morris dancing and singing in the marketplace.

Right: **May Day festival, 1950.** The arrival of spring is celebrated by dancing around a maypole decorated with flowers and ribbons.

LADYBOWER

Ladybower is the largest of the three reservoirs in the Derwent Valley. In 1943, while under construction, it was used for practice runs for the Dambusters and later used as the location for the film of the same name.

ABOVE: The villages of ASHOPTON and DERWENT – the "lost villages of Derbyshire" – were submerged under the waters of the Ladybower Dam. In periods of drought it is still possible to see the remains of Derwent village.

RIGHT: **ASHOPTON POST OFFICE, 1936.** Postmaster William Hubbard built his rustic post office single-handedly from local stone. He is seen here discussing its impending doom with a local man. The village disappeared under the waters of the dam in 1945.

ABOVE: **LADYBOWER RESERVOIR, SEPTEMBER 1945.** This photograph was taken shortly after the opening of the reservoir, a ceremony which was performed by King George VI. The reservoir was built at a cost of £6m to meet the needs of Sheffield, Derby, Nottingham and Leicester. In the right foreground of the picture is the viaduct carrying the diverted road from Ashopton to Bamford. In the distance can be seen the viaduct for the famous road over the Snake Pass into Lancashire.

RIGHT: **DERWENT HALL, MARCH 1925.** This fine stately home was built by Henry Balguy in 1672 and extended in the 19th century. It was acquired by the Derwent Valley Water Board in 1927 and served as a youth hostel and school for a few years before stripping and demolition began in 1942. Together with the hall, other buildings in the villages which were submerged included the Ashopton Inn, the Methodist Chapel and the church. The bodies from the graveyard were re-interred at Bamford.

BAKEWELL, ASHFORD AND THE CENTRAL PEAK

The Central Peak, with its wooded valleys and gentle contours, is a welcoming contrast to the exposed uplands of the High Peak.
Ashford-in-the-Water and Bakewell are at the centre of this region, on the beautiful river Wye.

ABOVE: **ASHFORD-IN-THE-WATER.** Sheepwash Bridge, over which sheep were flung to clean their fleeces before shearing, must be one of the most photographed spots in this idyllic village. Located just two miles north-west of Bakewell, Ashford was famous for the black marble so beloved by the Victorians for fireplaces, vases and jewellery. Many of the stone cottages in the village served as workshops for its production before the marble works were established by a Bakewell man, Henry Watson, in 1748.

LEFT: Building a drystone wall, 1941. The ancient craft of "stone-walling" is vital to the landscape of the Central Peak where drystone walls – which are built without the benefit of mortar – take the place of hedges in other parts of the country.

ABOVE: **BAKEWELL.** This photograph, taken in the 1930s, shows the large parish Church of All Saints and the medieval bridge over the River Wye. The largest town within the Peak District National Park, Bakewell is today a bustling centre for traffic and tourists. There is much to attract visitors – the famous Monday market, glorious mellow stone buildings (including the Old Town Hall, now the Tourist Information Centre of the Peak District) and the Old House Museum, which has been restored by the Bakewell Historical Society.

RIGHT: **EYAM,** the "plague cottage" and the church of St Lawrence. The village of Eyam, five miles north of Bakewell, will live forever in the collective memory as the place where the local inhabitants sealed their village off from the outside world in order to prevent the spread of the plague, which reached them in 1665. A tailor, George Viccars, was lodging in the cottage of Mary Cooper (foreground, right) when he received a parcel of cloth from London. As it was damp on its arrival, the cloth was hung in front of the fire to dry. It must have been infected with the plague bacillus, because Viccars became ill and died a few days later. The local rector, William Mompesson, persuaded his terrified parishioners not to flee. They stayed put – parcels of food were left for them on the village boundaries – but paid a terrible price: around 250 people died, including Mary Cooper's two sons and Catherine Mompesson, the rector's wife.

The country house

The Central Peak is the location of two of Britain's most important stately homes – the romantic and mysterious Haddon Hall on the river Wye and the splendid Chatsworth House on the Derwent. Both have been owned by the same families for generations.

ABOVE: **HADDON HALL, 1858.** A Victorian gentleman in a top hat gazes in awe at the entrance to this rambling mansion. The Hall, which dates from 1170, is set among trees and pastures on a knoll above the river Wye, one mile south of Bakewell. It is unique in that it combines elements from the later middle ages and from Tudor times, yet while it was meticulously maintained it was largely untouched in the 18th and 19th centuries. The building is reputed to be the first fortified house in England. It has been the ancestral home of the Dukes of Rutland for more than 800 years; legend has it that in 1558 Lady Dorothy Vernon eloped from the house on horseback with Sir John Manners, inspiring the 1927 film *Dorothy Vernon of Haddon Hall*, starring Mary Pickford. Whether or not the legend is true, heraldic symbols in the form of topiary representing the Vernon and Manners families embellish the splendid terraced gardens.

RIGHT: An aerial view of **HADDON HALL**. It is only when you view the house from above that the true scale of it is appreciated.

ABOVE: **CHATSWORTH HOUSE**, *c1875.* This pastoral scene was captured by Richard Keene (1825-1894) of Derby. He made several photographic tours of the Peak District, trundling his equipment around in a specially-constructed handcart, and Chatsworth was one of his favourite subjects. The present house is largely the creation of the Duke of Devonshire who, between 1686-1707, re-modelled the original house – built by the formidable Bess of Hardwick and her second husband William Cavendish – and turned it into a fabulous Palladian mansion. In the years between 1569 and 1584 Mary Queen of Scots was held prisoner at Chatsworth on several occasions and some rooms in the house are still referred to as the "Queen of Scots Apartments". Not only is Chatsworth a treasure house of works of art and antiques, but its superb "natural" setting was achieved by the 18th-century gardener Lancelot "Capability" Brown who swept away the formal gardens and replaced them with today's open, natural-looking landscape.

RIGHT: **IN THE GARDENS**, **1955**. Visitors descend the Lion Steps and the pathway through the Salisbury Lawns leading to the foot of the Cascade. At this time the house was not occupied by the family but it and the gardens were open to the public on a regular basis.

TRAILS AND DALES

The limestone plateau which is at the heart of the Peak National Park contains several glorious dales – among them Miller's Dale, Lathkill Dale, Tideswell and Monsal Dale – now a popular footpath and cycle track.

ABOVE: **MILLER'S DALE, c1950.** This tiny hamlet, seven miles east of Buxton, was built in the 1860s to provide housing for the workers who were building the London-Manchester railway line. The railway has now gone, a casualty of the rail closures of the 1960s, but the track has been incorporated into the Monsal Trail. This long-distance footpath runs the length of the dale and has a glorious riverside walk along the Wye. It incorporates the dramatic Monsal Dale viaduct.

RIGHT: **MILLER'S DALE, 1936.** The postman climbs a steep hill to deliver the mail. At this time, the village still served as a junction on the line to Buxton, bringing visitors into the Peak District.

ABOVE: **TIDESWELL**, *c1950*. This small market town is on the river Wye six miles east of Buxton. The 14th-century parish church of St John the Baptist is known as "the Cathedral of the Dales" and is the finest in the Peak District. It was built during the town's heyday as a centre for lead-mining and sheep-farming. Today the town is a useful starting point – and watering hole! – for the Monsal Trail.

BELOW: **MONYASH**, *c1950*. The ancient farming village of Monyash is situated at the head of Lathkill Dale, considered to be the most beautiful of the Derbyshire Dales. Its 18th and 19th-century houses are clustered around the village green and pond, the Fere Mere. This is fed by an underground spring and was used by villagers as a source of drinking water and for watering cattle.

MATLOCK AND THE SOUTHERN PEAK

The southern part of the Peak District is famed for its scenic gorges, which include Dovedale, together with many important sites from its industrial past.

ABOVE: **VIA GELLIA, BONSALL,** *c*1890. A dreamy view of the via Gellia and the Pig of Lead Inn, near the village of Bonsall. Situated two miles south of Matlock in a steep-sided dale, Bonsall was famous for its lead-mining and textile mills. Via Gellia is the road between Grangemill and Cromford; it was given its romantic name by the local industrialist, Philip Gell, shortly after the road was built. The name, slightly altered, was later adopted by Coats Viyella and used as a brand name for their famous soft cloth.

RIGHT: **LEAD PICKING IN THE SNOW, 1909.** "Pigs" of lead (ingots) have been found in Britain since Roman times. Fourteen occur in Ashbourne where, in 1288, the earliest mining laws were recorded. Derbyshire's lead-mining region is called "the King's or Queen's Field". It is governed by its own ancient legal system, the Barmote courts.

RIGHT: **PIT BOYS, 1912.** The arrival of a "cinematographer" arouses interest at this mine in the Derbyshire coalfield.

RIGHT: **WINSTER, 1952.** "Earth tremor rocks village" was the headline on February 23 1952 when Winster, south of Matlock, was shaken by two violent earth tremors. Ceilings partly collapsed, masonry and chimneys crashed and ornaments were shaken from walls. Most of the villagers rushed into the streets and, while many had a narrow escape, none was injured. Here, people look at fallen masonry from a chimney stack.

MATLOCK

ABOVE: **MATLOCK, 1907.** Traffic warily negotiates the streets of the town after the river Derwent broke its banks in October 1907. Over time, this has been a common occurrence; on the bridge near the bandstand there are plaques which record some of the high water marks.

RIGHT: **MATLOCK BATH, 1907.** The May Day parade winds its way through the picturesque village of Matlock Bath. One mile south of Matlock, it was here that the spa developed which gave rise to the town's prosperity. The wooded hillside in the distance is called The Heights of Abraham, a name chosen by the local people to commemorate General Wolfe's victory at Quebec. The narrow gorge of the Derwent was said to resemble the gorge of the St Lawrence river, to the north of which are the original Heights of Abraham.

RIGHT: **ROYAL VISITATION, 1933.** The Duke of York (later King George VI) visits the John Smedley Mills in Matlock.

ABOVE: **MATLOCK, 1936.** A bus pulls away from snowy Matlock, heading towards Cromford and Wirksworth. Cromford is famous the world over as the site of the first water-powered cotton mill; today the village, mill buildings and a 15-mile (24km) stretch of the Derwent Valley from Matlock Bath to Derby are an International World Heritage Site. It was the great industrialist, Richard Arkwright, who saw the potential of the fast-flowing waters of the Derwent – in so doing, he helped usher in the Industrial Revolution.

Ashbourne goes mad!

Each spring the small town of Ashbourne hosts one of the oldest sporting fixtures in the world – Royal Shrovetide Football. Hundreds participate, the goal is three miles apart and some of the action takes place in a river. No wonder there have been many attempts to ban it!

ABOVE: **LET BATTLE COMMENCE, 1928.** It was in this year that the Prince of Wales (later King Edward VIII) "turned up" the ball to start the match and gave the game its royal accolade. Here crowds watch as the ball is "kicked-off" in the waters of Henmore Brook. The players are formed of two teams – the Up'ards and the Down'ards – depending on which side of the river they were born. As the goals are three miles apart, at Sturston and Clifton (both on the south side of the river) much of the action takes place in the water.

LEFT: **WATER FOOTBALL, 1961.** More than three decades later the scene is repeated further upstream.

LEFT: **BATTLE BALL, 1952.** The ball at the centre of the game is a very special object, with a new one manufactured every year. Made of leather and filled with cork, to help it float, the ball is decorated with scenes particular to the dignitary or local person who starts, or "kicks off" each game. On both days the games are preceded by lunch, starting at 12pm at the Green Man Hotel. In 2003 the game on Ash Wednesday was "kicked off" by the Prince of Wales.

BELOW: **ON THE HOME STRAIGHT, 1952.** The game has few rules and takes place in the river, along the roads of the town and out into the fields of the surrounding countryside. When the ball gets within striking distance of the goalpost, leading players, usually drawn from a handful of well-known local families, draw lots as to who "goals" it. Women can take part – in 1943, Doris Mugglestone became the first woman to goal a ball.

DOVEDALE

One of the loveliest valleys in England, the little limestone gorge of Dovedale adjoins the grounds of Ilam Hall.

ABOVE: **DOVEDALE, 1936.** A visitor rests on a drystone wall overlooking the river Dove.

ABOVE: **DOVEDALE, 1950.** Looking down river from the stepping stones, one of the most photographed spots in the Peak District.

RIGHT: **ILAM HALL, 1935.** This fine Gothic mansion was built by the industrialist Jesse Watts Russell in the 1820s. In 1934 it was bought by Sir Robert McDougall JP, who presented it to the National Trust for use as a youth hostel. Today, Ilam Hall retains its country house atmosphere and its beautiful grounds contain formal Italian gardens and a Paradise Walk which runs alongside the River Manifold. It is a perfect base for exploring Dovedale.

WELL-DRESSING

TISSINGTON, 1923. Children look at at a recently-dressed well. This ancient rite takes place on Ascension Day, the fifth Thursday after Easter. The custom flourishes in the Peak District, with Tissington, four miles south of Ashbourne, its most famous exponent. The rite probably has its roots in the Celtic past, when it was customary to make offerings to water spirits; in the Middle Ages the villagers of Tissington gave thanks to their five wells for sparing them from the Black Death. Today, the custom has a Christian flavour and the pictures which adorn the wells usually have biblical themes. Six wells are dressed: the Hall, the Town, the Yew Tree, the Hands, the Coffin and the Children's Well.

First published in 2009 by Myriad Books Limited
35 Bishopsthorpe Road, London SE26 4PA

Photographs copyright Getty Images
Text © copyright Myriad Books Limited

ISBN 1 84746 259 6

Designed by Jerry Goldie

Printed in China